NARCISIA

Juana Castro

Translated by Ana Valverde Osan

Printed in the United States of America

Juana Castro

Narcisia

Translated by Ana Valverde Osan

ISBN: 978-1-60801-086-8

Library of Congress Control Number: 2012934232

University of New Orleans Press
unopress.uno.edu

Acknowledgements

I would like to thank two of my friends and colleagues, Alan Barr and George Bodmer, professors of English in the Department of English at Indiana University Northwest, for the careful reading they did of my translation of this book. Also, I am also very grateful to Juana Castro, for her patience and for the time she spent with me answering the many questions I had. My sincere thanks to all three of them.

Contents

INTRODUCTION

Written by Juana Castro in 1986, Narcisia is among the many long poems that were published in Spain in the last quarter of the twentieth century. They were a part of the blossoming of women's poetry that occurred after Franco's death in 1975. It was also the first of Juana Castro's two long poems; she followed it with *Del color de los ríos* (*The Color of Rivers*) in 2010.

In the midst of all the important awards that were given to women's books and the journals that were created to promote the literature by women in Spain during the 1980s, it seems surprising that their substantial contributions are not prominent in the contemporary anthologies of poetry. And they are similarly disregarded by the reviewers and critics. With the exception of a few articles and Biruté Ciplijauskaité's book, *Novísimos, postnovísimos, clásicos* (1990), the study of the poetry written by these women remains to be done.

Long poems emphasize a new perspective about women's ability to present their existence as a source of power and knowledge. With each new book, their vision of the female experience becomes, if not more complex, at least more ambitious and comprehensive. This is apparent in the evolution that began in 1985. Since then women writers no longer feel under the pressure of censorship, and they benefit fully from the liberalizing climate that is brought about by the French feminist movement of 1968 and the immediately following one in the Anglo-Saxon world. They are now able to deal with topics that had previously been considered taboo.

While *Narcisia* is born in this climate, Castro's strong consciousness about being a woman took place much earlier: as a child, she was very aware of the injustices than took place in the home. Furthermore, we could affirm that she perceived these injustices while still in her mother's womb, and that they came from her genes. Castro's mother, though not highly educated, was an intelligent woman who shared, intuitively, the most progressive ideas of American feminist women; atypically, she taught her daughter that a woman with economic independence had no need to get married.

These ideas remind us of the ones Virginia Woolf presents in *A Room of One's Own*, and also of those that Adrienne Rich would later develop in her essay, "Compulsory Sexuality and Lesbian Experience."   Upon examining economic, social, and historic factors, Rich concludes that "compulsory heterosexuality" has been fabricated by men to keep women under their control.   Moreover, she suggests that women, whether they are lesbians or not, move within a "lesbian continuum" that allows them to get in touch with other women under different facets that identify them as women, such as love, friendship, and solidarity, for example. I believe that Castro, who is a heterosexual, is located within this lesbian continuum as she perceives in lesbians the power of life and of regenerating strength in women. In a way that is similar to Rich's, Castro senses that under Franco's National Catholicism, the system in which she was socialized and educated, women were expected to be heterosexuals, in spite of the fact that, ironically, they were reared in a very contradictory way.

She states, "I have always felt a strong attraction to the female body, which was very logical, given the education we received regarding the male body. It just did not exist. What we used to see in the different paintings were naked women everywhere. We should have turned lesbians naturally, for that was how we were educated; however, we were persuaded to be heterosexuals."

Not only were women channeled into a sexual orientation that had been imposed on them, but they had to accept the legacy of a patriarchal God that assigned them to a subordinate state. Fortunately, the changes that took place with the advent of the feminist movement allowed for the resurrection of the primal goddess whose presence had been totally erased by the major monotheistic religions (such as Judaism, Christianity, and Islam.) Presently, the desire to reaffirm this old myth after more than five thousand years is an indication that the psyche needs to re-install this archetype.

The poet Amparo Amorós affirms that the new epic is a phenomenon with romantic roots; it expresses a desire to flee into heroic and ancestral worlds that will offer an alternative to the deep malaise in which we are born. Castro illustrates this tendency by going back to the beginning of time and by rescuing the ancient matriarchal goddess; this would alleviate the malaise in the inferior role to which women find themselves relegated. Castro's aims are of a double nature: on the one hand we perceive in her poetry the desire to reinstitute the goddess to offer women a symbol of independence, freedom, and energy, and on the other, there seems to be a desire to want to legitimate her divinity and to diminish the Christian myth's male figures of the Father, the Son, and the Holy Ghost. In this sense her attempt is deeply subversive, even sacrilegious; when she refers to her goddess, she re-appropriates the names and epithets that are used for Christ.

By replacing God the Father and the Holy Ghost with her feminine divinity, and her sensuality and sexuality, she subverts one of the most sacred myths of Christianity: that of Christ, Lamb of God, symbol of salvation. Re-conceiving the Christian precepts, Narcisia's divinity is deeply carnal, and her doctrine is exquisitely hedonistic. It becomes evident that the aim of the sexual act is not only reproduction but primarily pleasure.

Anthropologists and poets have long been theorizing about the existence of early matriarchal social orders; in 1861 Johann Bachofen published *Das Mutterrecht*, and later in the twentieth century, in 1948, Robert Graves made a splash with *The White Goddess*. More recently, Mary Daly has indicated that recent archeological and genetic discoveries back the idea of a primary goddess, and she brands as senseless the idea of identifying man with the original mother. Castro agrees; she notes that, even though the Catholic Church has never said it, "If women are the givers of life, the principle of creation in the world must be feminine."

Among the three epigraphs that head the book, two are by Saint Theresa and Saint John, two of the most important, applauded mystic poets. In Narcisia, Castro starts a dialogue with the latter, and she undertakes the rewriting of a love story. If in the past, mystic poetry may have appeared to be highly radical when applied to a heterosexual context, it turns into something bizarre and fantastic when presented within a bisexual one. Narcisia exhibits, in its 823 verses, many of the characteristics of long poems: it is divided into four cantos, a narrative thread unites the story that is presented, there is a dialogue with other texts, and there is no closure. More particularly, it avoids nostalgia; it highlights the voice of women's experiences that had been previously silenced, the celebration of the body, and the praise of sexual pleasure. Central to it are the permeability of the feminine "I" and the rejection of immortality. Everything contributes to the emergence of the primal goddess who has appropriated for herself the attributes of which she had been divested, and now she re-creates herself with greater strength than before.

Contrary to the myth of Narcissus, in which the young man dies while falling in love with his own image, Narcisia, while looking at and loving her own body, gives birth to her own reflection. With her, narcissism is a positive force for regeneration and self-identification that consolidates the relationships between women. Castro makes sure that the different stages of the patriarchal creation are clearly reflected, but they appear under a new perspective, for Narcisia does not issue any orders, or impose her will like the God of the Bible. She merely becomes a part of the episodes that are taking place. In this sense, she re-writes the ancient myth, and, at the same time, she sheds the old stereotypes.

In the poem "Paradise," Castro makes it a point to re-write the events that took place during the episode of the Fall in Genesis. Narcisia is in the Garden of Eden, alone and without Adam. There is a tree of life that is "beautiful and shiny," and we identify it with Narcisia, who is the fountain of all wisdom. There are no "apples" to bite, and the snake is abandoned at the end of the poem and kept isolated between parentheses. Even though Narcisia shares with the ancient goddesses many of their characteristics, Castro will try until the very end of the poem to dissociate her from the mythological goddesses of the patriarchal legacy.

As in his day the poet Vicente Huidobro would encourage other poets to become "little gods" by simply creating, Castro turns into one by giving birth to Narcisia and becoming a priestess for the goddess. Throughout, the harmony between Narcisia's body and nature is evident, and this close relationship becomes a new force that will question the patriarchal model that is always threatening everything. At a time when there is a sense of unhappiness that is caused by the confrontation between different systems and interests, Narcisia becomes a healing pool into which we can go and find solace. Castro's forward-looking modern epic encourages changes in the prevailing culture and in our present-day society.

—Ana Valverde Osan

NARCISIA

La mujer es la tierra misma llevada a la cima de la vida, la tierra vuelta sensible y dichosa.

- M. Carrouges

Otra manera de arrobamientos hay…

- Teresa de Jesús

¡O llama de amor viva,
que tiernamente hyeres
de mi alma en el más profundo centro!

- Juan de la Cruz

Woman is the land itself raised to the zenith of life, the land
turned sensitive and happy.

- M. Carrouges

There are other kinds of ecstasies…

- Teresa de Jesús

Oh, living flame of love,
that hurts tenderly
the most profound center of my soul!

- John of the Cross

Gloria

Apareció en el cielo una señal grande, una mujer
envuelta en el sol, con la luna debajo de sus pies,
y sobre la cabeza una corona de doce estrellas.

San Juan

Glory

A large sign appeared in the sky, a woman
wrapped in the sun, with the moon under her feet,
and on her head a crown of twelve stars.

Saint John

Inanna

Como la flor madura del magnolio
era alta y feliz. En el principio
sólo Ella existía.
Húmeda y dulce, blanca,
se amaba en la sombría
saliva de las algas,
en los senos vallados de las trufas,
en los pubis suaves de los mirlos.
Dormía en las avenas
sobre lechos de estambres
y sus labios de abeja
entreabrían las vulvas
doradas de los lotos.
Acariciaba toda
la luz de las adelfas
y en los saurios azules
se bebía la savia
gloriosa de la luna.
Se abarcaba en los muslos
fragantes de los cedros
y pulsaba sus poros con el polen
indemne de las larvas.
¡Gloria y loor a Ella,
a su útero vivo de pistilos,
a su orquídea feraz y a su cintura!
Reverbere su gozo
en uvas y en estrellas,
en palomas y espigas,
porque es hermosa y grande,
oh la magnolia blanca. Sola!

Inanna

Like the mature flower of the magnolia
She was tall and happy. At the beginning
only She existed.
Moist and sweet, white,
she loved herself in the dark
saliva of algae,
in the enclosed breasts of truffles,
in the soft pubises of blackbirds.
She slept amidst oats
over beds of stamens
and her bee lips
opened up the golden
vulvae of lotuses.
She caressed all
the light from the oleanders
and on the blue saurians
She drank the glorious
sap of the moon.
She embraced herself in the fragrant
muscles of cedars
and she pressed her pores with the undamaged
pollen of larvae.
Glory and praise to Her,
to her uterus alive with pistils,
to her fertile orchid and to her waist.
May her joy reverberate
in grapes and in stars,
in turtledoves and ears of wheat,
because she is great and beautiful,
oh the white magnolia. Alone!

Ser Inmóvil

Vestida de dalias,
al borde de la luz atraviesa los ojos.
Hasta el agua la siguen, y Ella hunde
la nata de sus pies en las miradas.
Evanescente blanca, de las dunas
somnolienta regresa, mientras crecen
violentos los jacintos.
Mil cristales de arena
tintinean violetas en sus brazos,
un espejo la carne, devuelta a su destello,
en Sí misma se hermana y se complace.
Ni la codicia, el miedo o la lisonja
podrían retenerla, ni erizarle siquiera
de su orla, el último hilo de la túnica.

Still Being

Dressed in dahlias,
at the edge of light She pierces eyes.
They follow her to the water, and She sinks
the cream of her feet before everybody's gaze.
Evanescently white, She returns
from the dunes sleepy, while the hyacinths,
violent, grow.
A thousand sand crystals
jingle violets in her arms,
the flesh a mirror, returned to its brightness,
She unites and pleases Herself.
Neither greed, fear nor flattery
could hold her, nor even make her bristle
out of her border, the last thread of her tunic.

Juana Castro

Causa Incausada

La noche de san juan,
en la hora más ciega se aparece
coronada de rosas, como una llama blanca.
¿A quién festeja, a quién
busca encendida, a quién,
lasciva y dulce, entregará su boca?
Los que la vieron, sueñan
con camelias azules estallando en las manos,
con bambúes fragantes y caobas y garzas.
Pero Ella, que mana de Sí misma
y a Sí propia regresa,
lleva en Sí todo el vino,
toda la miel, el heno, la salvia y los enjambres
florecidos en ojos y en caricias.
Con el alma en las manos
la Magna, la Dichosa, ferviente sobre atlas
atraviesa la tierra,
porque Ella es el mundo.

Cause Without Cause

The night of saint john,
She appears in the blindest hour
crowned with roses, like a white flame.
Whom does She celebrate, burning, whom
does She look for, to whom,
lascivious and sweet, will She surrender her mouth?
Those who saw her, dream
with blue camellias bursting in their hands,
with fragrant bamboos and mahoganies and herons.
But She, who flows from Herself
and returns to Herself,
takes in Her all the wine,
all the honey, the hay, the sage and the swarms
blooming in eyes and in caresses.
With the soul in her hands
the Great, the Happy one, passionate over atlas
She goes across the earth
because She is the world.

Victoria Regia

(Especie de nenúfar perteneciente
al grupo Ninfeáceas.)

Sobre el agua, los dedos no podrían
separar sus cien pétalos.
Podéis mirarla blanca, su corazón espeso
y los círculos verdes, escanciando
la linfa con el aire,
Oh Gran Diosa del lago,
lujuriante milagro el de su pulpa
de luna sosegada,
sobre su luz compacta se complace
y el color de la rosa, en su carne cerrada
se condensa. Oh, qué labios azules
morderían su cuerpo perfumado,
uno a uno el azúcar rosado de sus miembros,
sus rebanadas prietas, encendidas de malva.
Oh, qué tiempo perdido
de entreabrir su corola,
su rojo corazón
como un fruto de mar
regresado del fondo,
sangre ahogada brillante, comestible,
triunfadora granada del amor.

Royal Victory

(A species of water lily that
belongs to the nymphaeaceae family).

Over the water, fingers could not
separate her one hundred petals.
You may see her all white, her thick heart
and the green circles, pouring
the lymph with the air,
Oh Great Goddess of the lake,
that lusty miracle, her pulp
of a quiet moon,
she delights over her dense light
and the color of the rose, in her taut flesh
is condensed. Oh, that blue lips
would bite her scented body,
one by one the rosy sugar of her limbs,
her dark slices, lit up in mauve.
Oh, what time wasted
half-opening her corolla,
her red heart
like a fruit of the sea
returned from the bottom,
shiny drowned blood, edible,
triumphant pomegranate of love.

Aquaria

Llovía largamente por todos los rincones.
Gotas dulces llovían por su espalda,
miel de venas azules el cabello,
arco ciego del mar.
Nalga rosa perdida,
húmeda luz, la clara
porosidad de nieve de sus pómulos.
Arroyos, mar, cascadas inundando
los brazos y las cuevas,
golondrina en el borde su mirada.
Líquida llueve, líquida
se sumerge en las algas
y una rosa de yodo, como una ventana
le florece en la sangre.

Aquaria

It rained for a long time upon all the corners.
Sweet drops fell over her back,
her hair, honey of blue veins,
blind arc from the sea.
Lost pink buttock,
damp light, the clear
porosity of snow of her cheeks.
Streams, sea, cascades flooding
the arms and the caves,
a swallow at the edge of her eyes.
She rains liquid, liquid
she dives in the algae
and an iodine rose, like a window
blooms in her blood.

Domus Aurea

Andaba, y una estela
la seguía de huellas y de ojos.
Adonde la gacela,
quien su avispero dulce,
como su mar convulso de peonías.
Seguirla, seguirla hasta la orilla
de su ojiva de dátiles,
su tarazana muda
de gluten y de edelweiss.
Sitiar, sitiar su oscura poma
por ventanas y canas y dovelas,
descubrir los nectarios
de sus rosas gencianas
y arañar en sus vidrios
como un sol en la noche.
Oh las hidras, el viento,
alertas las mandrágoras conjurando las yucas,
si pudieran las redes
apacentar los copos
de las flores tan breves de la zarza,
respirar la clausura, el perfume de oro
de la albacora húmeda.
Oh, ebriedad, derribemos
las puertas, domeñar
la luna y la cellisca
y que la llaga sea
la dehiscencia en flor del relicario.

… "Pero Ella, abriéndose
su paso en la penumbra,
salió sobre las aguas,
su corazón mercurio crecido en el espejo,
como un adianto indemne".

Domus Aurea

She walked, and a trail
of footsteps and eyes followed her.
Toward the gazelle,
whose sweet wasps' nest,
like her ebullient sea of peonies.
To follow her, to follow her to the shore
of her ogive of dates,
her mute shelter
of gluten and edelweiss.
To besiege, to besiege her fruit
through windows and reeds and voussoirs,
to discover the nectaries
of her gentian roses
and to scratch her windowpane
like a sun at night.
Oh the hydras, the wind,
the mandragoras alert, conjuring the yuccas,
if the nets could
appease the bundle
of the ever so brief bush flowers,
breathe the closing, the golden perfume
of the humid albacore.
Oh, drunkenness, let us tear down
the doors, subdue
the moon and the sleet
and may the wound be
the blooming dehiscence of the reliquary.

…"But She, making
her way in the penumbra,
appeared over the waters,
her heart grown mercury in the mirror,
like an undamaged adiantum."

Juana Castro

Belle De Jour

Con las perlas, el oro y los brocados
elevaron un ídolo y amaron su hermosura.
Temblando, de rodillas,
su testuz adoraron, coronada,
con resinas ungieron su suavísimo lomo
y a la hendida pezuña
ofrecían las lilas y el espliego.
No la busquéis, la Bella, postrada en los altares
del benjuí y la plata
porque desprecia tintes, encajes y diademas.
Como un manso caloyo, se descalza en la hierba
y su carne refulge de diamante,
transparecida y libre.
No le ofrendéis ni sedas,
ni clámides ni lino,
porque ella es su oribe y sus alhajas.
Reclinada, su desnudo es un liquen
dulcemente esmeralda, más precioso
que el ruiseñor o el vuelo de la tórtola
y ni el rey salomón con toda su riqueza,
igualarla podría en la gloria
de sus ingles azules, como bayas de mirto.
Ni los lirios del campo, con su esplendor violeta
alcanzarían los tristes
corales de sus rótulas,
sus aréolas ácidas, la ambrosía
de su lento membrillo, sus talones
de mayo barnizados,
poco a poco el azúcar
de su fresa larvada, los rubíes
amor de sus amores, desnuda.

Belle De Jour

With the pearls, the gold and the brocades
erected an idol and loved her beauty.
Shaking, on their knees,
they adored her forehead, crowned,
they anointed resins over her very soft back
and to the cloven hoof
they offered lilacs and lavender.
Do not look for her, the Beautiful One, prostate over the
    altars
of benzoin and silver
because she despises dyes, laces and diadems.
Like a gentle lamb, she goes barefoot on the grass
and her flesh shines like a diamond,
transparent and free.
Do not offer her silk,
nor capes nor linen,
because she is her limit and her jewelry.
Leaning, her nude is a
sweetly emerald lichen, more precious
than the nightingale or the flight of a turtledove
and neither king solomon with all his wealth,
could equal her in the glory
of her blue groin, like myrtle berries.
Nor the lilies of the fields, nor her violet splendor
could reach the sad
corals of her kneecaps,
her bitter areolas, the ambrosia
of her slow quince, her heels
varnished in May,
slowly the sugar
of her hidden strawberry, the rubies,
love of her loves, naked.

Juana Castro

Sedes Sapientiae

Pueden todos dormir.
Ahora es Ella en la noche
y va su dulce lengua
a recorrer los pliegues más inciertos.
Como un ave, se tiende
sobre sus propias plumas
y está la opacidad
desgranándose lenta por sus codos.
Nocturnamente el agua
asciende en las acequias
y su nido derraman las palmeras
sobre el ojo despierto de las garzas.
Dormid, dormid, durmientes bellos.
Ella, la Gran Despierta, abre
su abadía de amor contra la luna.
Se deleita, yacida sobre el vaho
fluyente de los sueños
y en su ensenada vive
plenamente mojada
de dulzura.

Sedes Sapientiae

They can all sleep.
Now it is She in the night
and her sweet tongue goes
over the most uncertain folds.
Like a bird, she lies
over her own feathers
and opacity slowly
comes unstrung through her elbows.
Nocturnally water
rises in the waterways
and the palm trees spill their nest
over the herons' alert eye.
Sleep, sleep, beautiful ones.
She, the Great Awakened One, opens
her abbey of love against the moon.
She takes delight, lying over the flowing
vapor of dreams
and in her cove she lives
fully drenched
in sweetness.

Juana Castro

Aeterna Laetitia

No hay dolor en su mano.
Riente, se despeña
cantando por su cuerpo
como el abrazo verde de la draba.
Del cielo a los tobillos
derramada canéfora,
todo el placer granado de los mundos,
en su umbela de pozo se convoca.
Bienhadada, se goza de su sangre
rosa y tibia de acacia
y pasea desnuda sin espinas
por el oasis rojo de su nuca.
Ella es la Gran Dea, la Gloriosa
tañedora de anémonas,
la más acaudalada que pudieran
—mientras la angustia crece en los narcisos—
sonar los horizontes.
Ella, la que su oído ama sobre todas las cosas
y guarda en su cintura
una sima de estrellas,
la que cubre su carne
del licor de rocío
que le mana la boca.

Aeterna Laetitia

There is no pain in her hand.
Smiling, she falls off
singing through her body
like the draba's green embrace.
From heaven to her ankles
spilled canephora,*
all the important pleasure of the worlds,
convenes in the well of her umbel.
Fortunate, she enjoys her pink and lukewarm
acacia blood
and she walks around naked without thorns
through the red oasis of her nape.
She is the Great Dea, the Glorious
player of anemones,
the wealthiest one that
—while the anguish grows among the narcissuses—
the horizons could play.
She, who loves her hearing above all things
and who keeps on her waist
an abyss of stars,
the one who covers her flesh
with the dew's liqueur
that flows out of her mouth.

* In ancient Greece, each of the maidens who carried on
their heads baskets bearing sacred objects used at certain
feasts.

Juana Castro

Gratia Plena

Cual un tallo, curvada, de gramíneas
sobre su flor copiosa se derrama,
Salve Amor, genital
Ginecea de la gracia
dulce alondra de su plumón doblada.
Sacra larva bermeja, de su Vida
la Verdad y el Camino.
Rendidos corporales sus pestañas
sombreadas o estigmas,
de oro verde el racimo de sus óvulos.
Salve llama fecunda,
Ella es sola consigo,
rosa de Jericó, bendita
sobre el cedro y la vid.
Cubierta con su sombra, por los siglos
su lujuria purísima
en corolas rodando y arrayanes.
Salve grávida espiga,
patena de oración en su pistilo
beben vida los mundos, y en su vientre
una ubérrima flor, como una herida,
en su pasión se abre,
oh vencida piedad.

Gratia Plena

Like a stem of grasses, curved,
she spills herself over her luxuriant flower,
Hail Love, genital
Gyneceum of grace
sweet lark folded on her down.
Sacred red larva, of her Life
the Truth and the Way.
Her shaded eyelashes are tired corporals
or stigmas,
green gold her bunch of ovules.
Hail fertile flame,
She is alone with herself,
rose of Jericho, blessed
over the cedar and the vine.
Covered with her shadow, through centuries
her most pure lust
rolling around on corollas and myrtles.
Hail pregnant spike,
paten for prayer, in her pistil
the worlds drink life, and in her womb
a fertile flower, like a wound,
opens up in her passion,
oh vanquished piety.

Agnus Dea

Cuando Diosa la Altísima pasaba
por las calles henchidas de inmundicia y de lepra,
enfermos y lisiados le tendían las manos, suplicantes.
Era el aire hervidero de ruinas y llagas
y no había una brizna de verdor en la tierra.
Pero ella pasaba.
Como jazmín pasaba, alba tersa y balsámica,
y a su paso los juncos y el agua florecían.
Bienaventurados los rotos, porque Ella
es lozana y blancura.
Como begonias rojas, hematíes
hermosos destilaba
y melisas y olivas de su bulbo.
Gozo y paz de sus ácidos, la gloria
dispersa de sus ojos,
joyas ya las heridas por la senda
azul de sus muñecas.
Intacta curación la que sembraban
su inmarchitable plasma,
su córnea y su saliva.
En el filo de té de su vestido
ven la luna los ciegos
y la herida tan larga sobre el ara
resplandece y se cierra, fervorosa.
Como palma pasaba, y a su paso
en la luz se inundaban los abismos.
Y abriéndose los cielos, una dulce paloma
de la Inmortal Cordera se posaba en las sienes.

Agnus Dea

When Goddess the Highest passed
through the streets full of squalor and leprosy,
the sick and the crippled extended their hands, begging.
The air was seething with ruins and wounds
and there was no single blade of green on earth.
But she went by.
She went by like a jasmine, smooth dawn and balsamic,
and on her way the reeds and the water flowered.
Happy are those who are broken, because She
is wholesome and white.
Like red begonias, she distilled
beautiful red cells
and melissas and olives from her bulb.
Joy and peace from her acids, the scattered
glory of her eyes,
jewels already the wounds through the blue
path of her wrists.
Intact cure that were sowing
her unwithering plasma,
her cornea and her saliva.
In the border of tea of her dress
the blind see the moon
and the long wound over the altar,
fervent, shines and closes down.
She went by like a palm, and on her way
the abysses would flood in the light.
And with the heavens opening up, a sweet dove
from the Inmortal Ewe alighted on her temples.

Regina Pacis

Con rizoma de lirio se peina frente al sol
y una paloma dulce le vuela por las manos.
Está el bosque sangrando por recoger sus ojos
y Ella en su pelo vive.
Solamente en su pelo, tamarindo
de luz adelgazada.
Crece un rumor de manos vegetales
y cuando la clepsidra
agoniza de sed en su cristal,
arde ya el monipodio
con sus garras perdidas en los sauces.
La clemátide alarga
sus dedos venenosos, escanciando
peligrosos anillos de sátiros y sirenas y ninfas.
El algazul la llama
a sus flores hidrópicas de diosa
y los chopos, mentirosos obscenos,
le ofrendan su alta sombra
para amarla más mínima.
Sus esporas al vientre, a la miel de la luna
van los lactarios mansos
y el rubio corazón
vocea la matricaria, compasiva matrona.
El ciclamen estalla
sus coronas de estrellas carmesíes
y los diegos de noche le arrojan sus mil velos
cuando zeus, centauro de abedules,
en su aliento derrama adormideras sacras.

… Mientras Ella, Providencia Impasible,
como un cerezo en flor, desnuda con sus huesos,
sus cabellos conoce y se demora
dulcemente peinándose,
pues sabe que ninguno
podrá ser arrancado sin que su asenso sea.

Narcisia

Regina Pacis

With the rhizome of an iris she combs her hair in front of the sun
and a sweet dove flies over her hands.
The forest is bleeding to pick up her eyes
and She lives in her hair.
Only in her hair, tamarind
of thin light.
A rumor of vegetal hands grows
and when the clepsydra
agonizes with thirst on its crystal,
the monopodium burns already
with its claws lost in the willows.
The clematis lengthens
its poisonous fingers, pouring
dangerous rings of satires and mermaids and nymphs.
The carpetweed calls her
 to her hydropic goddess flowers,
and the poplars, obscene liars,
offer her their high shadow
to love her even smaller.
Her spores go to her womb,
the gentle lactariuses to the honey of the moon
and the blonde heart
shouts at the matricaria, compassive midwife.
The cyclamen bursts
its crown of crimson stars
and the four o'clock flowers throw at it their thousand veils
when zeus, the centaur of birch trees,
in his breath spills sacred poppies.

… While She, Impassible Providence,
like a cherry tree in bloom, naked with her bones,
knows her hair and takes her time
brushing it softly,
for she knows that not one
will be pulled without her consent.

Juana Castro

Ofertorio

Has dado cuerpo al aire y voz a los otoños. En ti repasa el mundo sus edades de fiebre, halla razón de sí, tiene memoria y canto. Todos se salvarán para que tú los salves.

FRANCISCO GARCÍA MARQUINA

Offertory

You have given body to the air and a voice to autumns. In you the world goes over its ages of fever, finds a reason for itself; it has memory and song. They will all save themselves so that you may save them.

FRANCISCO GARCÍA MARQUINA

Mater Fidelis

Ella es Hermosa.
Cristal embelesado de Sí misma,
no la toca el amor.
Desceñida de todo,
como la escarcha rueda su indolencia,
en los ojos un glaciar extrañado,
azul el pliegue que le desmaya el copo,
hiedra o helecho, sándalo, flor o frío.
Cubil de su mirada,
en la oscura camelia se detiene y ensimismada pasa
como un alud de hastío.
Nevisca del verano
al exilio dorado de su cuerpo,
oh tánatos en flor, mortal Narcisia.

Mater Fidelis

She is Beautiful.
Crystal enraptured with Herself,
love does not touch her.
Unbound from everything,
she rolls her indolence like frost,
in her eyes a surprised glacier,
blue the crease which the flake faints on her,
ivy or fern, sandalwood, flower or cold.
The lair of her look,
she stops in the dark camellia and pensive she goes on
     like an avalanche of boredom.
Summer snowfall
to the golden exile of her body,
oh thanatos in flower, deadly Narcisia.

Vas Spirituale

Tan sólo en su cristal
vive y espera.
Inútil, un violín
le adelgaza la flor
yerta y mar del oído.
Tres gotas de rocío,
sus diez yemas sapientes,
la última camisa de la última muda
y todas las heridas de las alas.
Aunque la amara el sol
y le enviara un ramo de gardenias de encaje
y fuera el arcoíris pulsera de la luz en sus tobillos,
Ella no ha de mirar
sino el hondo entramado de sus ojos.

Vas Spirituale

Only in her crystal
does she live and wait.
Useless, a violin
shrivels the rigid
flower and the sea of her ear.
Three drops of dew,
her ten wise fingertips,
the last shirt of the last change of clothes
and all the wounds on her wings.
Even if the sun loved her
and sent her a bouquet of lace gardenias
and the rainbow were the bracelet of light on her ankles,
She is not to look
but at the deep framework of her eyes.

Juana Castro

Turris Eburnae

La perla más oculta
se derrama en su boca.
Crecida de su almíbar
—Mirad como se ama—
la más dulce blandura
le hace nido en las palmas si se pulsa
y guarda, de topacio, sus mil ojos
para sola mirarse.
Posesa de Sí misma,
cada palmo de piel es una rosa
que seráficamente abarca. Abraza,
gózase contemplada
como una Venus tibia,
amante la más tierna,
la más sensual vampira
sobre su carne propia libándose la luz,
circular hermosura destilada
que sólo de Sí crece,
saúco inagotable,
ígnea valva en la miel.

Turris Eburnea

The most hidden pearl
spills out in her mouth.
Grown on her syrup
—Look at how she loves herself—
the sweetest softness
makes a nest in her palms if she feels the pulse
and keeps, of topaz, her thousand eyes
to look at herself alone.
Possessed of Herself,
each piece of skin is a rose
that she encircles seraphically. She embraces,
She enjoys herself being contemplated
like a soft Venus,
the kindest lover,
the most sensual vampire
sipping light over her own flesh,
circular beauty distilled
that only grows from Her,
inexhaustible elder,
igneous valve in honey.

Juana Castro

Sanguinis

Mieles o luz, sangraba
y en sus manos exprimía los tréboles
como pequeños pájaros exhaustos.
De azul hierro la brecha
tercamente incesante.
Condensado sigilo la ventura
de abrir negra la flor desde el abismo
y esperar a que el tiempo,
como un ganglio de niebla aquiete su desorden.
Con sus venas abiertas, las Danaides
derretidas se abaten
y hay un mar con arándanos
goteantes y vivos.
Trufas de amor, en tierra
como riñones trágicos o lirios.
Vuelve ciega la noche
y se desangra el mar.
Y Ella duerme y expira.

Sanguinis

She was bleeding, honey or light,
and in her hands she squeezed the clovers
like small exhausted birds.
The iron blue gash
incessantly stubborn.
Condensed stealth, the fortune
of opening the black flower from the abyss
and waiting for time,
like a ganglion of fog to quiet down its disorder.
With their veins open, the melted
Danaids swoop down
and there is a sea with blueberries
dripping and alive.
Truffles of love, in land
like tragic kidneys or lilies.
Blind, the night returns
and the sea bleeds.
And She sleeps and dies.

Juana Castro

Orchis Purpurea

Irresistible lenta, se acaricia
hasta el rigor tensada.
Trasoñar de la carne, ansiosa limitando
su tesoro lunar,
devorador del espejismo la pupila.
Por la pradera inmensa
se deslizan los dedos lentamente,
ofrendadas la cera y la penumbra.
Desfallecida sed, como si un ojo,
toda la magma espera
la fundación veraz bajo su tacto,
la estilizada forma
después de que su forma la vacíe.
Y la mano vacila. Pero sólo los ojos
se derraman temblando
blandamente en la herida.
Anaranjada y nácar, la masa de la carne
como un rayo fulgura.
Invisibles lebreles
el aliento se espían en el aire.
Llamándola, la doble llamarada
de los muslos de plata, la garganta,
el cristal de los senos como un lirio,
la lánguida planicie de su vientre
y la confusa orquídea despeinada.
Ella, por siempre Ella,
la Gran Narcisia blanca
amándose en la luz, idolatra
su mano, prensadora y ardiente.
Imantada la abeja, circular
en gozo y en lascivia,
tejedora en la flor,
eterna boca.

Orchis Purpurea

Slowly irresistible, she caresses herself
rigorously tense.
The flesh dreaming, limiting anxiously
its lunar treasure,
the pupil devouring the mirage.
Throughout the immense prairie
the fingers slowly slide;
wax and penumbra were offered.
Weak thirst, as an eye,
all the magma waits for
the true foundation under its touch,
the stylized form
after its shape empties it.
And the hand hesitates. But only her eyes
spill out softly
shaking in the wound.
Orange and mother-of-pearl, the mass of flesh
flashes like thunder.
Invisible greyhounds
spy on their breath in the air.
Calling her, the double blaze
of the silver thighs, the throat,
the crystal of her breasts like a lily,
the languid plain of her womb
and the confused orchid, disheveled.
She, forever She,
the Great Narcisia, white,
loving herself in the light, she idolizes
her hand, pressing and hot.
The magnetized bee, circular
in joy and in lascivia,
weaver in the flower,
eternal mouth.

Juana Castro

Mortalis Rosa

La miraban, balanceando tenue
un dolor en los álamos.
Abril se derramaba
en muerte y alhelíes.
Por sus senos, coronados de escarcha,
ha transido el dolor
y han cesado mil veces sus arterias.
Si sus tibias, como plata se encienden en la noche,
es su boca la luna,
amargo cáliz lleno
de atravesar amargos novilunios.
Preciosa sangre blanca
prendida de sus párpados,
por espinas de agua su cintura
tachonada de eclipses.
Hermosísima Tánatos, verbena
cien veces regresada de las sombras,
gloria dulce sus lágrimas, el júbilo
mecido de su encaje, la íntima
delectación gozosa de sus tarsos.

Mortalis Rosa

They would look at her, softly swinging
a pain on the poplars.
April was spilling out
in death and wallflowers.
Through her breasts, crowned with frost,
pain has struck
and a thousand times her arteries have stopped.
If her tibias, like silver, light up at night,
her mouth is the moon,
a bitter sorrow filled
with going through bitter new moons.
Precious white blood
fastened on her brows,
through thorns of water, her waist
dotted with eclipses.
Most Beautiful Thanatos, verbena
a hundred times returned from the shadows,
sweet glory her tears, the rocked
joy of her lace, the intimate
joyful delight of her tarsuses.

Juana Castro

Stella Matutina

Avanza, segura entre las mieses,
desnuda con su piel.
Paladea la brisa
delgada de las cañas
y el crepúsculo enciende
crisantemos violetas en sus ojos.
Atrás queda el olimpo
y sus lejanos dioses recostados
en su tiempo de gloria.
Todo ya languidece.
Las fumarias expiran
su ruinoso fulgor entre las tapias
y han depuesto sus yelmos el laurel y el acanto.
Ella sola en el éter.
Solamente el perfil
de sus sienes de oraje.
El racimo dorado de su espalda
y sus vanos hermosos,
los hundidos alvéolos,
branquias de rosas dulces.
Ella, sola lunaria,
final caleidoscopio para el éxtasis
de hacia dentro morir
transitando el ustorio que es su cuerpo
rendido entre los pétalos.

Stella Matutina

She goes forth, sure of herself among the cornfields,
naked with her skin.
She tastes the thin
breeze of the canes
and dusk turns on
violet chrysanthemums in her eyes.
Mount olympus remains behind
and its leaning far-away gods
in their time of glory.
Everything languishes.
The fumarias expire
their ruinous glow between the walls
and laurel and acanthus have laid down their helms.
She alone in the ether.
Only the profile
of her temples of storm.
The golden bouquet of her back
and her beautiful openings,
the sunk alveoli,
branchiae of sweet roses.
She, the only lunaria,
the final kaleidoscope for the ecstasy
of dying inside
going through the burning glass which is her body
worn-out among the petals.

Helianthus

Entre sus manos tiembla
de amarse extenuada,
cuánta yacida carne
de oro en el reguero
albo y dulce del vino.
En las piernas agrestes y en los brazos
le maduran las drupas.
Desmayadas estrellas
le atardecen la línea
en espiral de lluvia decrecida.
Una amapola pálida
es su útero exangüe.
Tulipanes y féculas a Ella,
al girasol ardiente de su boca.
Violenta en el rocío,
fidelísimos vidrios le sangran la cintura
y en su regazo breve,
consumida oquedad para los bosques,
se muere ya la lengua
de la vincapervinca
azul donde su cuerpo,
remoto de dulzuras,
ameriza y umbría y languidece.

Helianthus

In her hands she shivers
exhausted from loving herself,
all lying flesh
of gold in the white and sweet
trail of wine.
On her rustic legs and on her arms
drupes ripen.
Fainted stars
end her spiral
line of diminished rain.
Her bloodless uterus
is a pale poppy.
Tulips and starches to Her,
to the burning sunflower of her mouth.
Violent in the dew,
very loyal glasses bleed her waist
and in her short lap,
worn away cavity for the forests,
the tongue of the blue
periwinkle
dies already where her body,
with remote gentleness,
lands on the sea, and darkens, and languishes.

Juana Castro

59

Nymphae Alba

Abierta. Abierta y amarilla
con sus labios vaciaba
todo el licor en trance de los ríos.
Devotamente, iba
deslizando corolas por sus miembros
y sus vanos sin aire,
disueltos y ceñidos, como una ventana
saturaban su cuerpo. Sabiamente
con sus labios bebía
y abrevaba los pétalos.
Hoz de miel en la boca,
cuando la lluvia vuelva, o el infierno,
la encontrarán envuelta, comenzando
a extenuarse libre.
Eterna quedará, abatida y violenta.
Beber. Beberse pálida. Sorberse.
(A la orilla los juncos) Ella es sola en el beso.

Nymphae Alba

Open. Open and yellow
with her lips she emptied
all of the ecstatic liqueur from the rivers.
Devotedly, she went on
sliding corollas through her arms
and her openings without air,
dissolved and tight-fitting, like a window
saturated her body. Wisely
with her lips she drank
and she gave water to her petals.
A scythe of honey in her mouth,
when the rain returns, or hell,
they will find her wrapped up, starting
to exhaust herself free.
She will remain eternal, disheartened and violent.
To drink. To drink herself pale. To sip herself.
(At the edge the canes)   She is alone in the kiss.

Rosa Mystica

Derribada, como amígdalas dulces
de genista se rompían sus huesos.
Era otoño y placer.
En borbotones rojos, la catalpa
su cabellera viva tendía sobre las vides.
Madroños de licor el de sus labios
hendidos en los gajos de la niebla y la luz.
Rosa y mortal, un campo era de oro
su carne bajo el peso discontinuo del sol.
Rosa y oral, toronja derramada
de la lengua a la lila,
tortura del enjambre desolado en su sed.
Sabed que bebe sangre
azul de limoneros,
que transporta un manojo
de fresas dormecidas,
que todas las delicias
sufren muerte de amor en sus ojeras.
Rosa de las rosas,
tribulación tan pálida sus pétalos
transidos de langor,
blanda astenia de duelo translucida,
exangüe deleitada
su hermosura final.

Rosa Mystica

Knocked down, like the sweet tonsils
of a retama plant, her bones would break.
It was fall and pleasure.
In red bubbles, the catalpa tree
hung her living hair over the vines.
Tree strawberries of liqueur that of her lips
cracked in the slices of fog and light.
Rose and deadly, her flesh was a field of gold
under the discontinuous weight of the sun.
Rose and oral, spilled grapefruit
from the tongue to the lilac,
torture of the desolate swarm in her thirst.
Be aware that she drinks blue
blood from lemon trees,
that she carries a bunch
of sleepy strawberries,
that all delights
suffer a death of love in the rings under their eyes.
Rose of roses,
such a pale tribulation her petals
overcome with languor,
soft, translucent asthenia of mourning,
bloodless delighted
her final beauty.

Bina Pulchra

Se amaban como líquenes
y traían estigmas liliáceos en los ojos.
Pero nadie las vio.
Sólo hierbas tronchadas, algún rastro
de miel en las ortigas,
jirones de un encaje
prendido en los beleños.
Sólo voces y trinos,
gemidos naufragados de la noche en los flancos,
aullidos de las lobas
sobre el jalde racimo de las lentibularias.
A ungirse de albahaca, de rocío y benjuí,
pasan raudas de pomas en la lengua
y cuando el sol acora, delirante,
los palpos de la araña,
Ellas huyen al agua con sus trenzas
y en las acequias hunden el fuego de sus ninfas.
Hacia el musgo dorado se vuelven de la noche,
a la verde tintura de su espejo,
al baobab inmenso de su gula,
cosechados geranios en las crines.
Nadie sabe sus nombres, su voz ni sus latidos.

Son un cuerpo, un dolor
de incensario en la drusa,
la Géminis total que en su Tabor se ama,
la bicromada biela tañida en soledad.

Bina Pulchra

They loved each other like lichens
and they brought liliaceous stigmas in their eyes.
But nobody saw them.
Only chopped grasses, some traces
of honey on the nettles,
shreds from lace
fastened on henbanes.
Only voices and trills,
the night's shipwrecked moans on the sides,
the howls of the she-wolves
over the yellow bunch of the lentibularias.
To be anointed with basil, dew and benzoin,
they pass currents of apples on the tongue
and when the sun, delirious, attacks
the spider's receptors,
They flee to the water with their braids
and in the waterways they sink their nymphs' fire.
Towards the golden musk they return from the night
to the green dye of their mirror,
the immense baobab of their gluttony,
harvested geraniums on the manes.
Nobody knows their names, their voice or their heartbeats.

They are one body, one sorrow
of incense on the druse,
the entire Gemini that loves herself in her Tabor,
the bicolor guitar played in solitude.

Gineceo

Amó tanto su cuerpo, que el espejo del mundo
le devolvió su imagen en miríadas.
Como a hoja leve de la albizia,
copiosamente alzábase su amor,
inagotable orgasmo en marabú y en rosa.
Lamida de leopardo, su dulce levadura
atravesó los siglos y los trenes,
humedeció las flautas y los salmos
y en las alcobas blancas, los faroles
de cera desleían los cíngulos.
Erógenas pavesas acariciaron Lesbos
y en un horno de estrellas se anegaban las malvas.
Bajo palio, violetas las mejillas
de Safo la sagrada, con aceite y alheña
sobre sus dedos, unge
las blusas derramadas de cerezas y nísperos.
Livideces de corzas, amazonas en flor,
como venas de ánades su gloria
vertida en la Vía Láctea
por frutales glicinas, por sedales y clítoris.

Gynaeceum

She loved her body so much that the mirror of the world
returned her image in myriads.
Like the light leaf of the albizia,
her love would rise copiously,
inexhaustible orgasm in marabou and in pink.
Leaked by leopards, her sweet yeast
went through centuries and trains,
it dampened the flutes and the psalms
and in the white rooms, the wax
lanterns untied the cords.
Erogenous embers caressed Lesbos
and in an oven of stars the mallows drowned.
Under a canopy, with the violet cheeks
of Sappho the sacred, with oil and henna
on her fingers, She anoints
the blouses spilled with cherries and medlars.
Lividities of does, amazons in flower,
her glory like the veins of ducks
spilled in the Milky Way
through wisteria orchards, through fishing lines and
      clitorises.

Misterios Eleusinos

Como Deméter dea, la dorada,
sus poros enfrutece
cuando sume su mano vaginal en la tierra
y alufrada se muestra, goteante
de amentos y fucsias.
A Eleusis la blanca,
de novísimos granos los cabellos,
harinosa la falda en el soplo del viento,
iban Io la negra,
Aretusa y Niobe,
la veloz Atlanta,
de frambuesas la boca cuajada de Aragné,
Castalia la purísima vencida de rocíos,
Como un dardo Talía
y Mnemosina triste, la de los ojos pétalos.
Cuando todas penetren
y agárico su alba de silencio,
le ofrecerán con mirra y cabrahigos
la pulsión libadora de su leche,
una espiga de trigo recogida en la calma,
su deliriada sangre de peonías,
seducción y misterio,
en catarsis de arándanos sus incisivos místicos
al rito del amor, al numínico ágape
de fraccionar, cantando,
como tiranas dulces
los virginales lienzos
de Su radiante Bulbo.

Eleusinian Mysteries

Like Demeter dea, the golden one,
her pores bear fruit
when she sinks her vaginal hand in the earth
and she shows herself briefly, dripping
aments and fuchsias.
Towards Eleusis the white one,
her hair of the newest grains,
her skirt, floury in the gusty wind,
Io, the black one, would go,
Aretusa and Niobe,
speedy Atalanta,
the mouth curdled with raspberries, Aragne,
Castalia, the most pure one conquered by dews,
Like a dart, Talia,
and sad Mnemosyne, the one with petal eyes.
When they all walk in
and her dawn of silence, an agaric,
they will offer her myrrh and wild figs
the sipping swelling of her milk,
a spike of wheat picked up in tranquility,
her delirious blood with peonies,
seduction and mystery,
in a catharsis of blueberries, her mystical incisors
to the rite of love, to the numinous agape
of fractioning, singing,
like sweet tyrants
the virginal cloths
of Her radiant Bulb.

Introito

¿Quién es ésta que se levanta como la aurora,
hermosa cual la luna,
resplandeciente como el sol,
terrible como escuadrones ordenados?

CANTAR DE LOS CANTARES

Introit

Who is this one who rises like dawn,
who is beautiful like the moon,
resplendent like the sun,
terrible like ordered squadrons?

THE SONG OF SONGS

Génesis

Era el líquido y bruma, y no había
luminarias ni gestos.
Sobre el agua, apacible,
se cernía su Aliento, y en el agua.
Hermosa y viva ya,
infusoria del cielo, amorosa y terrible.
Con flagelos de seda y de dulzura
se embellece y dispersa.
Lleva una boca dulce, cineraria
santísima en su masa de estrellas temblorosas.
Devota clavellina que serpea y acrece
su ternaria bondad.
Ella era la luz.
Su voz, por los espacios,
vibrátil transitaba, como cilios,
inaugurando esporas y crisálidas.
En Ella está el verbo.
Solipsisma del mar, alfa y omega
su vorticela cálida, protozoaria
malva, gloria in excelsis,
a su custodia eterna las fresas y los aloes,
azaleas y plata en sus pestañas,
el ámbar y las moras a su violento ojal.

Genesis

It was liquid and fog, and there were no
lights nor gestures.
Over the water, peaceful,
her Breath hovered, and in the water.
Beautiful and already alive,
infusoria from the sky, loving and terrible.
With whippings of silk and kindness
she becomes beautiful and disperses.
She has a sweet mouth, most holy
cinerary in her mass of shaky stars.
Devout carnation that creeps and increases
its ternary kindness.
She was the light.
Her voice, through spaces,
travelled quivering, like cilia,
inaugurating spores and chrysalises.
The verb is in Her.
Solipsism of the sea, alpha and omega
her warm vorticella, mauve
protozoan, gloria in excelsis,
to her eternal monstrance, strawberries and aloes,
azaleas and silver on her eyelashes,
amber and mulberries on her violent breach.

Juana Castro

Ginandria

Rotundo, un abismo le habita en la garganta
y en su útero el viento
convive con la luz.
Viaja a otra Ítaca más dulce
de duelo y soledad,
donde su cuerpo es tierra prometida.
Al principio, solamente fue el caos.
Totalidad de estrellas y raíces,
de tinieblas y plata la plural
contradicción oculta de su frente,
la alquimia de sus plantas con anémonas,
la herética dual de sus mejillas.
Magia, placer y miedo
a Ella, a la inquietud
de ojiva de su vientre
emanándolo todo porque el mundo
es su gozo de amarse en las axilas.
Dispersión, azucenas y ausencia
a su onírica fronda,
al idilio de rito con sus hombros,
a sus tiernas rodillas en el dédalo
de millares de imágenes,
catalizada tierra en sus ojeras,
mientras todos los seres
de Sí propia y su espejo se levantan,
en su bráctea nevada se confortan
y viven.

Gynandria

Resounding, an abyss lives in her throat
and in her uterus the wind
lives together with the light.
She travels to a sweeter Ithaca
of mourning and solitude,
where her body is promised land.
At the beginning, there was only chaos.
A totality of stars and roots,
of darkness and silver, the plural,
hidden contradiction of her forehead,
the alchemy of her plants with anemones,
the heretic duality of her cheeks.
Magic, pleasure and fear
to Her, to the ogival restlessness
of her womb
with everything emanating because the world
is her joy of loving herself in the axilae.
Dispersion, lilies and absence
from her oneiric foliage,
to the idyllic rite with her shoulders,
to her soft knees in the daedalum
of thousands of images,
land catalyzed in the circles under her eyes,
while all beings
out of Her and her mirror get up,
in her snow-covered bract they comfort each other
and they live.

Pruna Aurea

Dedales de cristal, sonreía inmutable
entre la zarza en llamas.
Dulces lenguas lamiendo
sus golondrinas hondas,
tropical fervor como los labios.
Ascuas de miel su carne con asfixia,
inalterable eterna
en plenitud caudal.
Inútilmente orfeo
con su lira desciende a los abismos
y dante en las tinieblas
se adentra, combustible.
Ella es el infierno.
Abismada y febril,
un almíbar de oro crepita en su ababol,
sangre pólvora y vida,
encendido azabache la gehena
de sus riscos impávidos.
De volframio radiante sus arterias,
todo el alba del fósforo en sus ojos
y la malva sevicia de su frente.
Ella sola es el fuego, los racimos
rosados de la zarza,
Ella es ígnea y acero, fosforescente y negra,
pozo rubio sus flancos,
serpentinas de exceso.
Impertérrita y aura,
licor gualda o estaño,
por guedejas desciende de petunias y guindos
y con sus brasas prende
toda la faz del mundo.

Pruna Aurea

Crystal thimbles, immutable, she smiled
among the burning bush.
Sweet tongues licking
her deep swallows,
tropical fervor like lips.
Her flesh embers of honey with asphyxia
unalterably eternal
wealthy in plenitude.
Uselessly, orpheus
with his lire descends to the abysses
and dante penetrates
in the darkness, combustible.
She is hell.
Sunk into an abyss and feverish,
a golden syrup crackles in its poppy,
powdery blood and life,
blazing jet the gehenna
of her fearless cliffs.
Her arteries of radiant volfram,
the entire dawn of phosphorus in her eyes
and the mauve brutality of her forehead.
She alone is the fire, the bush's
pink bunches,
She is igneous and steel, phosphorescent and black,
her sides a blond well,
streamers of excess.
Impassive and aura,
weld liqueur or tin,
through long hair she descends from petunias and
	sour cherries
and with her embers she sets on fire
the entire face of the earth.

Juana Castro

El Paraíso

Camino de la arena, por el árbol pasaba
y era hermoso y brillante.
Como el musgo terso, la reciente
verdura de sus hojas,
su deliriante tronco, y azulada
de lujuria su sombra o novilunio.
(Todavía sus ojos miraban hacia fuera)
Era el centro del mundo, la gloria del Edén
aquel árbol de fuego, redondeces
lascivas sus pomos entreabiertos
como caobas pálidas o clivias.
Sirena la serpiente, con su canto de trébol
inspiraba aquel sueño detenido en sus ramas.
Mas un día de otoño, con azafranes vivos
estallando en la tarde, hubo un mar
de hojas nítidas regalando cristales
en la lluvia.
Como onzas de plata,
los limbos repetidos la copiaban, hermosa.
Y fue Ella, radiante,
la que encendió de espejos su figura,
clara prímula inmensa, devorando
la desnudada imagen de su cuerpo.
Amar, extrema amarse, glauca, con los ojos,
bellamente invertidos, en la endrina
recóndita del vientre,
granada ya la mano, demorada
sobre el húmedo azul de su colmena.
Como una palmera, soberbia con sus hombros,
se alejaba en la noche,
las pestañas cuajadas
de alhelíes y dátiles.
(Mientras, flamígero,
eternamente sólo, la serpiente
llamaba)

Paradise

On the way to the sand, she went by the tree
and it was beautiful and shiny.
Like the smooth moss, the recent
greening of its leaves,
its delirious trunk, and its shadow
of blueish lust or moon.
(Her eyes still looked towards the outside)
It was the center of the world, the glory of Eden
that tree of fire, lascivious
roundnesses are its half-open apples
like pale mahoganies or clivias.
The snake is a mermaid, with her song of clover
she inspired that dream held in its branches.
But on a fall day, with living saffrons
bursting in the evening, there was a sea
of clear leaves giving away crystals
in the rain.
Like ounces of silver
the repeated limbuses copied her, beautiful.
And it was She, radiant,
who lit up with mirrors her figure,
clear, immense primula devouring
the naked image of her body.
To love, to love oneself extremely, glaucous, with the eyes
happily inverted, in the hidden
blackthorn of the womb,
the hand already with grains, late
over the humid blue of her beehive.
Like a palm tree, haughty with her shoulders,
she went away into the night,
her eyelashes full
of wallflowers and dates.
(In the meantime, the one on fire,
eternally alone, called
the snake)

Juana Castro

Mater Intemerata

Donde confluye el círculo estelar
con el abismo; donde es terrible el borde
y blanco, y dulce, y rojo. Allí donde el infierno
limita en querubines.
Allí se baña Ella,
desconocida agalla oval y cinamomo.
Al viento su mejilla
angélica se sabe y dracena en la música.
Desciende a las esferas y es salep
y mañana, y siempreviva y noche.
Esotérica y luz,
místico su cuerpo sabiamente
profundo y amansado,
abraza en sus encías
los astros y las trombas,
ritmo de niña y grande,
laberíntica eterna.
Aspira los espacios
con un prisma de fuego en arcoíris
y múltiple se goza, y varia, y viva.

(Mientras jorge, y miguel el arcángel,
persiguiendo dragones torvamente,
su corazón combaten y hermosura.)

Mater Intemerata

Where the stellar circle meets
the abyss; where the edge is terrible
and white, and sweet, and red. There where hell
is bound by cherubs.
There She bathes,
unknown oval gallnut and cinnamon.
In the wind her cheek
feels angelical and a dracena in the music.
She descends to the spheres and She is salep
and morning, and sempervivum and night.
Esoteric and light,
her body wisely mystical,
deep and tamed,
she embraces in her gums
the stars and the downpours,
the rhythm of a child and an adult,
eternal confusion.
She aspires spaces
with a prism of fire as a rainbow
and she enjoys herself manifold, and different, and alive.

(While george, and michael the archangel,
fiercely chasing dragons,
fight against her heart and beauty.)

Roca De Horeb

Y ya no tuvo sed.
Agónicas, algún rastro de agua
buscaban las panteras
y morían las águilas, volando
vanamente sangrientas a las nubes.
Enlazadas, las cobras perecían.
Con su ojo de piedra, dormitaban los pozos
y en vano los limones aspiraban su piel.
Las acequias cegadas y olvidadas las norias,
las espinas picaban los jilgueros
de las chumberas tristes,
enjuta la alta sierra
como panal en llamas.
Alocadas, de jaras y lentiscos
las raíces en rocas se rompían.
Solamente Ella Sola, la Innombrable
Serena, como un junco de mayo,
delicuescente tierna, laboraba un oasis
de geranios y bayas.
Y nunca tuvo sed.
Porque en mitad del fuego,
su almendra contenida se abrió como una ameba
y brotaron al punto cuatro chorros
de perlas. Manantial
de agua viva, para siempre saltando
ad vitam aeternam, desde Ella, amen.

The Rock Of Horeb

And she was no longer thirsty.
Agonizing, the panthers looked
for a trace of water
and the eagles died, flying
in vain to the clouds, bleeding.
Intertwined, the cobras perished.
With their eye of stone, the wells dozed off
and in vain the lemons sucked their skin.
The blind waterways and the forgotten waterwheels,
the thorns pinched the sparrows
from the sad trees,
the high sierra narrow
like a beehive in flame.
Wild, with rockroses and lentiscus,
the roots in the rocks were breaking.
Only She Alone, the Unnamable
Serene One, like a May reed,
softly deliquescent, she worked on an oasis
of geraniums and berries.
And she was never thirsty.
Because in the middle of the fire,
her contained almond opened up like an ameba
and at once four waterfalls of pearls
sprang. A spring
of living water, forever leaping
ad vitam aeternam, from Her, amen.

Speculum Justitiae

Como un espejo verde, su mirada
poseía los astros y las cosas.
De la luna al gentío, era su cuerpo
un fuego detenido.
Llama blanca en la noche, una cuerda
le sangraba los brazos,
exprimía sus pies
y se ahincaba, ascendiendo
por los pliegues iguales de la túnica
en su carne de avena.
Los jueces de alta toga
la divulgaron bruja
y ya en el palimpsesto estaba escrito:
"muerta hoy en la hoguera".
Que la leña, quizás, estuviera mojada,
o que fuera una flor incombustible.
Que su rara materia
sometiera la mecha como un nardo.
Lo cierto es que a la aurora
se vio ciega la pira, destrenzada
la maroma de esparto, como sirga vacía.
Cuando los jueces, en la catedral
rezaban los maitines,
un pájaro de plata, volando despiadado
por un rayo de luz, ascendido al triforio
salió por la archivolta, apresando en sus plumas
los ópalos y el iris, en el vitral dormido.

Speculum Justitiae

Like a green mirror, her sight
possessed the stars and things.
From the moon to the people, her body was
a detained fire.
A white flame in the night, a rope
bled her arms,
it squeezed her feet
and it sank, ascending
through the identical folds of the tunic
in her flesh of oat.
The judges of high toga
declared her a witch
and already on the palimpsest it was written
"burned today at the stake."
It could be that, perhaps, the wood was wet,
or that the flower was incombustible.
That its strange matter
would submit the wicker like a nard.
The truth is that at dawn
the pyre went blind, the esparto rope
unbraided like an empty towline.
When the judges prayed the matins
in the cathedral,
a silver bird, flying mercilessly
through a ray of light, ascended to the triforium,
went out through the archivolt, grasping in its feathers
the opals and the iris, sleeping in the stained-glass window.

Hipóstasis

Madurable amor y, pubescente,
le crecieron los bosques en la piel de los tilos.
Cantando, de nidos en cascada
goteó su garganta
y lactaron los peces
en sus mamas azules.
Como una llama roja,
de su pelo saltaron los océanos.
De sus ojos la arcilla, la roca y las arenas
densamente cubrieron el gozo de los campos
y en sus manos la luna
copió el arco rosado de su sueño.
El sol en su vagina
se incendió de naranjas
e inquietos los caballos, del tibio corazón
aprendieron el pulso.
Gorriones y corderos, acebos y secuoyas
empapados de Ella,
arroyos de su aliento
en estrellas y en nubes.
Fulgurante, por caderas y ovarios
resbalaba la lluvia.
Y cuando ya encendidos
de gloria en su regazo
florecían los mundos,
el más hermoso fruto le granó en lo más dentro,
en el hondo delirio de su arrebol amante.
Y se produjo el parto:
La perla más hermosa, la gota plateada
nacida de su estirpe, las más hermosa Hermana,
la Cumplida Dichosa
como una gota roja herida en las hortensias…

Hypostasis

Mature love and, pubescent,
the forests grew on the skin of linden trees.
Singing, her throat dripped
from cascading nests
and the fish nursed
on her blue breasts.
Like a red flame,
the oceans jumped out of her hair.
From her eyes the clay, the rock and the sands
densely covered the joy of the fields
and in her hands the moon
copied the rosy arch of her dream.
The sun in her vagina
was set ablaze with oranges
and the horses, restless, from her warm heart
learnt her pulse.
Sparrows and lambs, holly trees and sequoias
drenched in Her,
the brooks of her breath
in stars and in clouds.
Glittering, through hips and ovaries
the rain slid.
And when already lit
with glory on her bosom
the worlds flowered,
the most beautiful fruit grew deep inside her,
in the deep delirium of her beloved red.
And the delivery took place:
The most beautiful pearl, the silvery drop
born of her lineage, the most beautiful Sister,
the Perfect Happy One
like a red drop wounded in the hydrangeas…

Juana Castro

Apocalipsis

El espíritu del Valle no muere jamás:
se llama lo Misterioso Femenino.

LIBRO DEL TAO

Apocalypse

The spirit of the Valley never dies:
it is called the Mysterious Feminine.

THE BOOK OF TAO

Ella No Es Pomona.

Ni, como las Danaides,
una daga dorada oculta entre los senos.
Ella no es Calíope, aunque sea la voz y la belleza.
Y aunque, como las Náyades, ame fuentes y bosques,
no es Estigia ni Dafne
ni es la bella Afrodita
ni es sueño de los héroes.
Pero Ella ha nacido.
Como ananás fragante, se levanta
ungida de romero,
como custodia viva, derramando
cuatro copas dulcísimas:
Abrazo de la tierra,
música del aire,
luz violenta del fuego
y el almíbar del agua.
Ya no habrá nunca noche, porque Ella
se ha manifestado
con sus cuatro trompetas y su gloria.
Y así es la gran nueva, la alegría:
Porque Ella ha nacido
y esta es la señal, aleluya.
Que su gracia
sea con todos vosotros, aleluya.

She Is Not Pomona.

Nor, like the Danaids,
a golden dagger hidden between her breasts.
She is not Calliope, though she may be the voice and the
     beauty.
And even though, like the Naiads, she may love fountains
     and forests,
she is neither Styx nor Daphne
nor is she the beautiful Aphrodite
nor the dream of heroes.
But she is born.
Like a fragrant pineapple, she gets up
anointed with rosemary,
like a live monstrance, spilling
four very sweet cups:
The embrace of the earth,
the music of the air,
the violent light of fire
and the syrup of water.
Never again will there be night, because She
has manifested herself
with her four trumpets and her glory.
And thus is the great news, the joy:
Because She is born
and this is the sign, hallelujah.
May her grace
be with all of you, hallelujah.

Índice

Gloria

Ofertorio

Index

GLORIA

Inanna
Still being
Cause without cause
Victoria regia
Aquaria
Domus aurea
Belle de jour
Sedes sapientiae
Aeterna laetitia
Gratia plena
Agnus dea
Regina pacis

Offertory

Mater fidelis
Vas spirituale
Turris eburnea
Sanguinis
Orchis purpurea
Mortalis rosa
Stella matutina
Helianthus
Nymphaea alba
Rosa mystica
Bina pulchra
Gynaeceum
Eleusinian mysteries

Introito

Génesis
Ginandria
El Paraíso
Mater intemerata
Roca de Horeb
Speculum justitiae
Hipóstasis

APOCALÍPSIS

Ella no es Pomona

Introit

Genesis
Gynandria
Paradise
Mater intemerata
The Rock of Horeb
Speculum justitiae
Hypostasis

APOCALYPSE

She is not Pomona

Available from

uno PRESS

General Titles

The Not Yet by Moira Crone, 978-1-60801-072-1 (2012)

A Baltic Anthology Book 1: Contemporary Latvian Poetry, edited by Inara Cedrins, 978-1-60801-050-9 (2012)

A Baltic Anthology Book 2: Contemporary Estonian Poetry, edited by Inara Cedrins, 978-1-60801-052-3 (2012)

A Baltic Anthology Book 3: Contemporary Lithuanian Poetry, edited by Inara Cedrins, 978-1-60801-051-6 (2012)

**The Astral Plane: Stories of Cuba, the Southwest and Beyond* by Teresa Dovalpage, 978-1-60801-078-3 (2012)

**The Man Who Wanted to Buy a Heart* by Leonard S. Bernstein, 978-1-60801-073-8 (2012)

Post-Katrina Brazucas: Brazilian Immigrants in New Orleans by Annie McNeill Gibson, 978-1-60801-070-7 (2011)

New Orleans: The Underground Guide (2nd Edition) by Michael Patrick Welch & Alison Fensterstock, 978-1-60801-079-0 (2011)

The Saratoga Collection, edited by Terrence Sanders, 978-1-60801-061-5 (2011)

**The Garden Path: The Miseducation of a City*, by Andre Perry, 978-1-60801-048-6 (2011)

Before (During) After: Louisiana Photographers Visual Reactions to Hurricane Katrina, edited by Elizabeth Kleinveld, 978-1-60801-023-3 (2010)

**Beyond the Islands* by Alicia Yánez Cossío, translated by Amalia Gladhart, 978-1-60801-043-1 (2010)

**The Fox's Window* by Naoko Awa, translated by Toshiya Kamei, 978-1-60801-006-6 (2010)

Black Santa by Jamie Bernstein, 978-1-60801-022-6 (2010)

Dream-crowned (Traumgekrönt) by Rainer Maria Rilke, translated by Lorne Mook, 978-1-60801-041-7 (2010)

**Voices Rising II: More Stories from the Katrina Narrative Project* edited by Rebeca Antoine, 978-0-9706190-8-2 (2010)

**Rowing to Sweden: Essays on Faith, Love, Politics, and Movies* by Fredrick Barton, 978-1-60801-001-1 (2010)

Dogs in My Life: The New Orleans Photographs by John Tibule Mendes, 978-1-60801-005-9 (2010)

New Orleans: The Underground Guide by Michael Patrick Welch & Alison Fensterstock, 978-1-60801-019-6 (2010)

Understanding the Music Business: A Comprehensive View edited by

Harmon Greenblatt & Irwin Steinberg, 978-1-60801-004-2 (2010)

The Gravedigger by Rob Magnuson Smith, 978-1-60801-010-3 (2010)

Portraits: Photographs in New Orleans 1998-2009 by Jonathan Traviesa, 978-0-9706190-5-1 (2009)

*I hope it's not over, and good-by: Selected Poems of Everette Maddox by Everette Maddox, 978-1-60801-000-4 (2009)

Theoretical Killings: Essays & Accidents by Steven Church, 978-0-9706190-6-8 (2009)

*Voices Rising: Stories from the Katrina Narrative Project edited by Rebeca Antoine, 978-0-9728143-6-2 (2008)

On Higher Ground: The University of New Orleans at Fifty by Dr. Robert Dupont, 978-0-9728143-5-5 (2008)

The Change Cycle Handbook by Will Lannes, 978-0-9728143-9-3 (2008)

Us Four Plus Four: Eight Russian Poets Conversing translated by Don Mager, 978-0-9706190-4-4 (2008)

The El Cholo Feeling Passes by Fredrick Barton, 978-0-9728143-2-4 (2003)

A House Divided by Fredrick Barton, 978-0-9728143-1-7 (2003)

William Christenberry: Art & Family by J. Richard Gruber, 978-0-9706190-0-6 (2000)

The Neighborhood Story Project

New Orleans in 19 Movements by Thurgood Marshall Early College High School, 978-1-60801-069-1 (2011)

The Combination by Ashley Nelson, 978-1-60801-055-4 (2010)

Between Piety and Desire by Arlet Wylie and Sam Wylie, 978-1-60801-040-0 (2010)

The House of Dance and Feathers: A Museum by Ronald W. Lewis by Rachel Breunlin & Ronald W. Lewis, 978-0-9706190-7-5 (2009)

Beyond the Bricks by Daron Crawford & Pernell Russell, 978-1-60801-016-5 (2010)

Aunt Alice Vs. Bob Marley by Kareem Kennedy, 978-1-60801-013-4 (2010)

Signed, The President by Kenneth Phillips, 978-1-60801-015-8 (2010)

Houses of Beauty: From Englishtown to the Seventh Ward by Susan Henry, 978-1-60801-014-1 (2010)

Coming Out the Door for the Ninth Ward edited by Rachel Breunlin, 978-0-9706190-9-9 (2006)

Cornerstones: Celebrating the Everyday Monuments & Gathering

Places of New Orleans edited by Rachel Breunlin, 978-0-9706190-3-7 (2008)

The Engaged Writers Series

Medea and Her War Machines by Ioan Flora, translated by Adam J. Sorkin, 978-1-60801-067-7 (2011)

Together by Julius Chingono and John Eppel, 978-1-60801-049-3 (2011)

Vegetal Sex (O Sexo Vegetal) by Sergio Medeiros, translated by Raymond L.Bianchi, 978-1-60801-046-2 (2010)

*Wounded Days (Los Días Heridos) by Leticia Luna, translated by Toshiya Kamei, 978-1-60801-042-4 (2010)

When the Water Came: Evacuees of Hurricane Katrina by Cynthia Hogue & Rebecca Ross, 978-1-60801-012-7 (2010)

*A Passenger from the West by Nabile Farès, translated by Peter Thompson, 978-1-60801-008-0 (2010)

*Everybody Knows What Time It Is by Reginald Martin, 978-1-60801-011-0 (2010)

*Green Fields: Crime, Punishment, & a Boyhood Between by Bob Cowser, Jr., 978-1-60801-018-9 (2010)

*Open Correspondence: An Epistolary Dialogue by Abdelkébir Khatibi and Rita El Khayat, translated by Safoi Babana-Hampton, Valérie K. Orlando, Mary Vogl, 978-1-60801-021-9 (2010)

Gravestones (Lápidas) by Antonio Gamoneda, translated by Donald Wellman, 978-1-60801-002-8 (2009)

Hearing Your Story: Songs of History and Life for Sand Roses by Nabile Farès translated by Peter Thompson, 978-0-9728143-7-9 (2008)

The Katrina Papers: A Journal of Trauma and Recovery by Jerry W. Ward, Jr., 978-0-9728143-3-1 (2008)

Contemporary Poetry

Sheer Indefinite: Selected Poems 1991-2011 by Skip Fox, 978-1-60801-080-6 (2011)

Atlanta Poets Group Anthology: The Lattice Inside by Atlanta Poets Group, 978-1-60801-064-6 (2011)

Makebelieve by Caitlin Scholl, 978-1-60801-056-1 (2011)

California Redemption Value by Kevin Opstedal, 978-1-60801-066-0 (2011)

Dear Oxygen: New and Selected Poems by Lewis MacAdams, edited by Kevin Opstedal, 978-1-60801-059-2 (2011)

Only More So by Tony Lopez, 978-1-60801-057-8 (2011)

Enridged by Brian Richards, 978-1-60801-047-9 (2011)

The Ezra Pound Center for Literature

Modernism and the Orient, edited by Zhaoming Qian, 978-1-60801-074-5 (2012)

A Gallery of Ghosts by John Gery, 978-0-9728143-4-8 (2008)

The Poets of the Sala Capizucchi (I Poeti della Sala Capizucchi) edited by Caterina Ricciardi and John Gery, 978-1-60801-068-4 (2011)

Trespassing, by Patrizia de Rachewiltz, 978-1-60801-060-8 (2011)

*The Imagist Poem: Modern Poetry in Miniature edited by William Pratt, 978-0-9728143-8-6 (2008)